Mathalon Maps

Number Crunch Your Way Around the World

ASIA

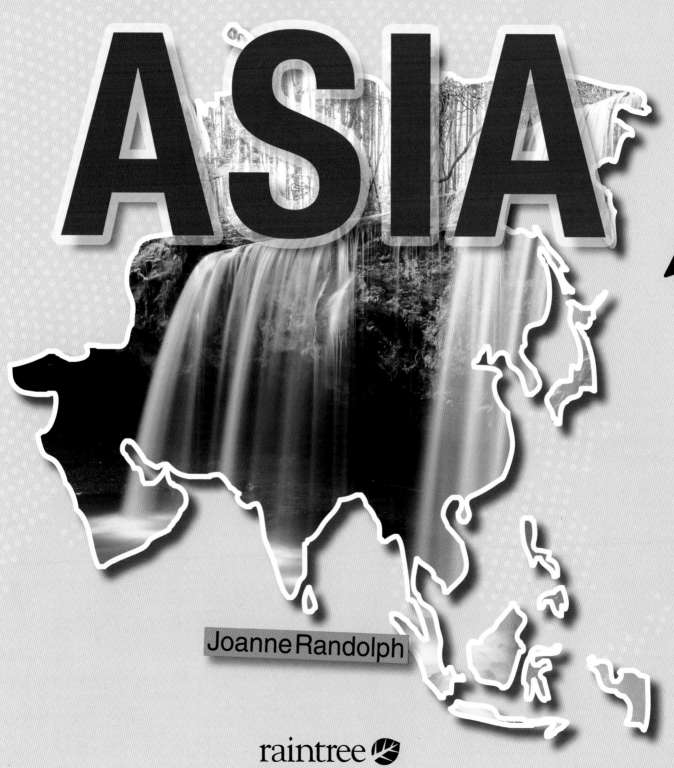

Joanne Randolph

raintree
a Capstone company — publishers for children

Raintree is an imprint of Capstone Global Library Limited, a company incorporated in England and Wales having its registered office at 264 Banbury Road, Oxford OX2 7DY – Registered company number: 6695582

www.raintree.co.uk
myorders@raintree.co.uk

Produced for Raintree by Calcium
Edited by Sarah Eason and Katie Woolley
Designed by Paul Myerscough
Illustrations by Moloko88/Shutterstock
Picture research by Sarah Eason
Production by Victoria Fitzgerald
Originated by Capstone Global Library Ltd © 2016
Printed and bound in China

ISBN 978 1 4747 1593 5
19 18 17 16 15
10 9 8 7 6 5 4 3 2 1

British Library Cataloguing in Publication Data
A full catalogue record for this book is available from the British Library.

Acknowledgements
We would like to thank the following for permission to reproduce photographs: NASA: 9tr; Shutterstock: 13r, Akiyoko 19b, Galyna Andrushko 12t, ChameleonsEye 23b, Chungking 7t, 29tr, Neale Cousland 24t, 26b, Ethan Daniels 17r, Pierre-Jean Durieu 15r, Ekipaj 25r, Jorg Hackemann 5b, ID1974 20t, Incredible Arctic 6c, Joppo 21r, KishoreJ 27b, Perati Komson 18tr, 28l, Sergey Krasnoshchokov 15t, Philip Lange 23t, LeonP 7r, Fuyu Liu 27t, Xidong Luo 25c, Mikhail Markovskiy 25b, Meiqianbao 10b, Dudarev Mikhail 17c, Vitalii Nesterchuk 22b, 29b, Norikazu 19r, Byelikova Oksana 16b, Zhukov Oleg 12b, Sean Pavone 4t, Pecold 14b, Vadim Petrakov 11l, Rawpixel 27r, Russal 20c, Skyearth 9b, Yury Taranik 8t, DK Tazunoki 1, 18b, Aleksandar Todorovic 17l, Nickolay Vinokurov 4b, WitthayaP 6b, Yuri Yavnik 5c; Wikimedia Commons: Guilhem Vellut 11t, 28tr.

Cover photographs reproduced with permission of: Dreamstime: Anton Sokolov (bottom), Ivan Varyukhin (top); Shutterstock: Yuri Yavnik (back cover).

Some words are shown in bold, **like this**. You can find out what they mean by looking in the glossary.

Contents

Asia

Asia is the world's largest continent, both in size and number of people. It also has the largest countries in the world, by size and population. Russia is the largest country on Earth by area. It is so large that part of it is found in Asia and part in Europe! China has the most people. Asia has the highest mountain and the lowest point on Earth, too. Are you ready to use your best maths and map skills to explore this giant continent?

How to use this book

Look for the "Map-a-stat" and "Do the maths" features and complete the maths challenges. Then look at the answers on pages 28 and 29 to see if your calculations are correct.

Osaka, Japan

Arctic Ocean

Pacific Ocean

Indian Ocean

the Dead Sea

4

A continent of differences

Asia is generally considered to have 48 countries. There is a huge difference between the **cultures**, **economies** and histories of all these places. Turkey, for example, lies at the crossroads between Europe and Asia. Its culture and economy are influenced by this location. The cultures of countries like India, Indonesia and Japan are all influenced greatly by their **geographies**.

Map-a-stat

The lowest point in Asia and the world is the Dead Sea, which borders Jordan and Israel. It is 418 m (1,371 ft) below sea level. It is also one of the saltiest places on the planet.

97 per cent of Turkey s in Asia.

Several countries in Asia were once part of the Union of Soviet Socialist Republics (USSR). They are Russia, Georgia, Uzbekistan, Tajikistan, Kazakhstan, Kyrgyzstan, Turkmenistan, Armenia and Azerbaijan.

the Great Wall of China

DO THE MATHS!

Use the information in red in the Map-a-stat box to work out the following challenge. How much of Turkey is in Europe? Here is the equation to help you solve the problem.

100 per cent - 97 per cent = ? per cent in Europe

Complete the maths challenge, then turn to pages 28—29 to see if your calculation is correct!

picking tea in Sri Lanka

What a continent!

Asia takes up 30 per cent of Earth's **landmass**, with an area of 44.6 million sq km (17.2 million sq miles). It has more than 4 billion people. Asia is connected to Africa by a narrow strip of land called the **Isthmus** of Suez. Asia borders Europe along the Ural Mountains and the Caspian Sea. It is surrounded on its other sides by the Indian Ocean, the Pacific Ocean and the Arctic Ocean.

Climate and weather

Asia has many different **climates**. It has warm, **tropical rainforests**, especially in the southeast and on some of its islands. It also has large, dry areas in the interior of the continent. Parts of Asia have a **monsoon season** and a lot of tropical **cyclones** affect its coastal areas. While much of southern Asia is very hot, Siberia is one of the coldest places on Earth. It has average daily temperatures of about -5 °C (23 °F) across much of the region, but it can be much colder in the winter and warmer in the short summer.

Reindeer live in the Arctic tundra in Russia.

This street in Ayutthaya, Thailand, has become flooded after a monsoon.

Map-a-stat

Of Asia's 4.4 billion people, 1.4 billion live in China and 1.2 billion live in India.

Seven out of the 10 most populated countries in the world are in Asia.

Asia has the longest coastline of any continent. The coast is 62,800 km (39,022 miles) long.

a colourful boat sails in Victoria Harbour, Hong Kong

DO THE MATHS!

Use the information in red in the Map-a-stat box to work out the following challenge. If 1.4 billion people live in China and 1.2 billion live in India, how many people live in the rest of Asia? Here is the equation to help you solve the problem.

$$4,400,000,000 \text{ people} - (1,400,000,000 + 1,200,000,000 \text{ people}) = ? \text{ people}$$

Orangutans live in Indonesia.

Complete the maths challenge, then turn to pages 28—29 to see if your calculation is correct!

Mountains

There are about 10 major mountain ranges in Asia and many smaller ones. The Ural Mountains form the border between Asia and Europe, stretching 2,500 km (1,550 miles) from northern Russia to Kazakhstan. The Altai Mountains form a range in east-central Asia that has a high point of 4,506 m (14,784 ft.). The highest peak in the Zagros, found in Iran and partly in Iraq, is 4,548 m (14,921 ft.).

Altai Mountains

Russia

Ural Mountains

Altai Mountains

Tian Shan Mountains

Kunlun Mountains

Zagros Mountains

China

Iran

Mount Fuji

Tallest peaks

The Kunlun Range runs across western China and along the Tibetan Plateau. Its tallest peak is Mount Muztagh at 7,723 m (25,338 ft.). The Tian Shan is in central Asia. Its highest peak is Victory Peak at 7,439 m (24,406 ft.) tall.

Himalaya Mountains

India

Ghats Mountains

Puncak Jaya

Map-a-stat

The Ghats in India are two mountain ranges. Their highest peak is Anai Mudi, which is 2,695 m (8,842 ft) tall.

Mount Fuji is a famous mountain in Japan.

It is 3,776 m (12,388 ft) tall. It is an active volcano near Tokyo, Japan's capital city.

The highest peak in the southwestern Pacific is Puncak Jaya at 4,884 m (16,024 ft) tall.

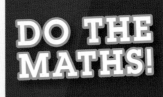

The Tian Shan Range, Asia, photographed from space

Mount Fuji can be seen from Tokyo, Japan.

DO THE MATHS!

Use the information in red in the Map-a-stat box to work out the following challenge. If you stacked the Ghats' highest peak on top of the highest peak in the Zagros Mountains (4,548 m), would the two mountains be taller or shorter than Victory Peak (7,439 m)? Here is the equation to help you solve the problem.

4,548 m + 2,695 m = ? m
Is that taller or shorter than 7,439 m?

Complete the maths challenge, then turn to pages 28—29 to see if your calculation is correct!

The Himalayas

The highest mountain range in the world is the Himalayas. It has more than 110 peaks that are over 7,300 m (24,000 ft.) high. The range runs through India, Pakistan, China, Bhutan and Nepal. The name Himalayas is a Sanskrit word that means "house of snow", and the range is named for its many snowy mountaintops. However, lower in the mountains, there are many different **habitats** that are home to all kinds of plants and animals. There are red pandas, musk deer and snow leopards, to name a few. There are also alpine meadows and forests.

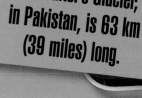

The Baltoro Glacier, in Pakistan, is 63 km (39 miles) long.

Tallest mountain

Mount Everest, on the border of Nepal and China, is the tallest mountain in the world. It stands 8,850 m (29,035 ft.) tall. It is also known as Chomolungma and Sagarmatha. Mount Everest brings people from all over the world who want to test themselves by trying to climb to its **summit**. It is a dangerous goal because around 250 people have died trying to climb the mountain.

Everest Base Camp

Map-a-stat

The sources of the Ganges River, the Indus River and the Brahmaputra River are all in the Himalayas. More than 1 billion people depend on the water from these rivers.

The Himalayas stretch more than 2,500 km (1,550 miles) across northeastern India.

When measured from its base beneath the ocean floor, Mauna Kea in Hawaii is even taller than Mount Everest, which measures 8,850 m (29,035 ft.). Mauna Kea measures around 10,200 m (33,464 ft.) tall. However, only 4,205 m (13,796 ft.) of the mountain are above sea level, which is why it is not considered the tallest mountain in the world.

Mount Everest's Tibetan name, Chomolungma, means "Mother Goddess of the Mountains".

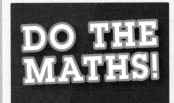

DO THE MATHS!

Use the information in red in the Map-a-stat box to work out the following challenge:

1) If Mount Everest and Mauna Kea were sitting next to each other on the ground, how much taller would Mauna Kea be?
2) How much taller is Mount Everest than Mauna Kea above sea level? Here are the equations to help you solve the problem.

$$1) \ 10,200 \text{ m} - 8,850 \text{ m} = ? \text{ m}$$

$$2) \ 8,850 \text{ m} - 4,205 \text{ m} = ? \text{ m}$$

Complete the maths challenge, then turn to pages 28—29 to see if your calculation is correct!

Deserts

Asia is home to many large deserts. The Arabian Desert takes up most of the Arabian Peninsula in the Middle East. It has an area of around 2.33 million sq km (900,000 sq miles). The Kyzylkum Desert straddles Uzbekistan and Kazakhstan. It gets between 10–20 cm (4–8 in) of rain per year. This rain falls during cooler weather. It provides water for many animals in the region, such as antelopes, deer and boars. The Karakum Desert makes up 70 per cent of Turkmenistan's land and has an area of 349,650 sq km (135,000 sq miles).

Gobi Desert

Kyzylkum Desert

Karakum Desert

Takla Makan Desert

Arabian Desert

Thar Desert

the Arabian Desert

Map-a-stat

China's largest desert is the Takla Makan Desert, which spreads more than 319,993 sq km (123,550 sq miles) across western China. It is a sandy desert with many sand dunes.

The Thar Desert in India is a **subtropical desert**. In some years, parts of the desert get up to 51 cm (20 in) of rain during the monsoon season.

On average, temperatures in the Gobi Desert can drop to -40 °C (-40 °F) in the winter. In the summer, temperatures can rise to a blistering 45 °C (113 °F).

The Gobi Desert covers parts of northern China and southern Mongolia.

Arabian horse

The Gobi Desert

The Gobi Desert is Asia's second-largest desert, after the Arabian Desert. It is a rain shadow desert. This means much of the rain it might get is blocked by the tall Himalayas and other mountain ranges. It still gets up to 20 cm (8 in) of rain, though. It is a rocky desert and has cold winters and hot summers.

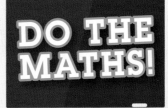

DO THE MATHS!

Use the information in red in the Map-a-stat box to work out the following challenge. What is the difference in temperature between the summer and winter temperatures in the Gobi? Here is the equation to help you solve the problem.

$$45\,°C - (-40\,°C) = 45\,°C + 40\,°C = ?\,°C \text{ difference in temperature}$$

Complete the maths challenge, then turn to pages 28—29 to see if your calculation is correct!

Tundra and steppes

Asia is home to the world's largest **steppe** region, called the Eurasian Steppe. A steppe is a **grassland biome**. The Eurasian Steppe starts in Europe and stretches in a wide belt across the whole continent of Asia, reaching as far north as Siberia.

tundra

Eurasian Steppe

The tundra

Asia's tundra is in the northernmost part of Russia. This is a very cold and windy place. Temperatures can reach as low as -50 °C (-58 °F) and the highs in summer are between 2.8–12 °C (37–54 °F). Little rain falls in the tundra. People still live in the tundra, despite the cold. Animals also live there, including reindeer, ermine and polar bears.

Some people in northern Russia tend herds of reindeer, living in tents and moving with their animals.

Map-a-stat

The Eurasian Steppe reaches nearly one-fifth of the way around Earth. It is about 8,047 km (5,000 miles) across.

The permafrost in Russia's tundra can be 1,524 m (5,000 ft.) deep.

Worldwide, tundra covers around 10 per cent of Earth's surface.

Reindeer eat lichens buried under the snow in winter, and grasses in the summer months.

There are more Mongolian horses in Mongolia than there are people!

DO THE MATHS!

Use the information in red in the Map-a-stat box to work out the following challenge. If the United States is around 4,828 km across, how much wider is the Eurasian Steppe? Here is the equation to help you solve the problem.

$$8,047 \text{ km} - 4,828 \text{ km} = ? \text{ km wider}$$

Complete the maths challenge, then turn to pages 28–29 to see if your calculation is correct!

Indonesia

Indonesia is an archipelago in southeast Asia. It is made up of thousands of islands. It has 30 provinces. By population, it is the fourth-largest country in the world, but only the fifteenth-largest by land area. Indonesia has about 17,500 islands, and about 10,500 of those have people living on them. The islands also have a lot of active volcanoes. The volcanic ash makes the soil very fertile, but eruptions have also killed many people over the years.

Pacific Ocean

Indonesia

Jakarta

Krakatoa

Tambora

Gas and ash spurt out of Krakatoa.

Volcanoes

Indonesia is known for its many active volcanoes. It has more than 100 active volcanoes, including Krakatoa and Tambora. Around 76 of these have **dated eruption reports**. While many have not erupted in hundreds of years, they are still considered active.

Jakarta is Indonesia's capital city.

Map-a-stat

When Krakatoa erupted in 1883, more than 36,000 people died as a result of the eruption and the **tsunamis** that followed.

Indonesia is the fourth-most populated country in the world, with a population of almost 254 million. However, its land area is only about one-fifth of the United States'.

Indonesia is one of the world's most **biodiverse** places. Tigers, rhinoceros, Asian elephants, orangutans, leopards and monkeys live in Indonesia. Many bird **species** and hundreds of **reptiles** and **amphibians** are found there, too.

the Wayag Islands, Raja Ampat, Indonesia

terraced rice fields in Bali

DO THE MATHS!

Use the information in red in the Map-a-stat box to work out the following challenge. If the United States has a population of around 318 million, how many more people live in the United States than live in Indonesia? Here is the equation to help you solve the problem.

$$318{,}000{,}000 \text{ people} - 254{,}000{,}000 \text{ people} = ? \text{ more people}$$

Complete the maths challenge, then turn to pages 28—29 to see if your calculation is correct!

Japan

Japan is another archipelago in Asia. It is often called the "Land of the Rising Sun". Around 80 per cent of Japan's land is mountainous. This land cannot be used for agriculture, nor can building take place there. This means that most of Japan's people are packed into the livable areas, mainly on the coast.

Russia

China

North Korea

South Korea

Japan

Tokyo

Tokyo

Ring of Fire

Japan is part of the Pacific Ring of Fire. It has more than 100 active volcanoes. Japan also experiences many earthquakes and tsunamis due to the movement of Earth's **tectonic plates** in this area. An earthquake in Tokyo, Japan's capital city, in 1923 killed 140,000 people. In 2011, Japan experienced a 9.0 magnitude earthquake, which is an extremely powerful and damaging earthquake. Despite these **geological** challenges, Japan has a strong economy and is one of the world leaders in science and technology and other industries.

This waterfall is near Aso, Japan.

Map-a-stat

Japan's land area is 364,485 sq km (140,728 sq miles) and its water area is 13,430 sq km (5,185 sq miles).

There are more than 9 million people living in Tokyo. It has the largest metropolitan area in the world.

The 2011 earthquake was so powerful it moved Japan's main island, Honshu, 2.4 m (8 ft.) to the east.

Hakuba, in Nagano, Japan, is a popular tourist destination.

harvesting tea leaves in Mitoyo Kagawa

DO THE MATHS!

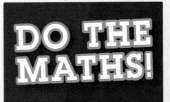

Clondalkin Library
Monastery Road
Clondalkin
Dublin 22
Ph: 4593315

Use the information in red in the Map-a-stat box to work out the following challenge. What is Japan's total area, including land and water? Here is the equation to help you solve the problem.

$$364,485 \text{ sq km} + 13,430 \text{ sq km} = ? \text{ sq km}$$

Complete the maths challenge, then turn to pages 28—29 to see if your calculation is correct!

Russia

Russia is a huge part of Asia. It has an area of 17.1 million sq km (6.6 million sq miles), which makes it the largest country in the world by size. It is only the ninth most populated country, though. Russia has around 142 million people.

Siberia

Siberia is a huge area in the northern part of Russia. It makes up more than 75 per cent of the country's land area, and yet only 27 per cent of the population lives in this region. This is due to the fact that Siberia can be a very hard place to live. It has short summers that are never very warm. It also has long, very cold winters.

the Trans-Siberian Railway

Siberia

Moscow

Russia

Oymyakon

Trans-Siberian Railway

Kazakhstan

Mongolia

Vladivostok

China

Map-a-stat

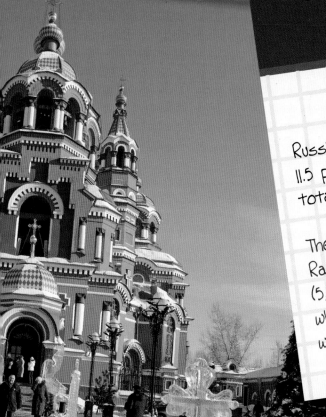

Russia takes up 11.5 per cent of Earth's total land area.

The Trans-Siberian Railway is 9,289 km (5,772 miles) long, which makes it the world's longest railway.

Oymyakon, Republic of Sakha, in Siberia, is listed as having some of the worst weather in the world. In 1933, it recorded a low temperature of -67.7 °C (-89.9 °F). Now, that is a cold place to live!

This temple is in Irkutsk, one of the largest cities in Siberia.

The laika is a breed of dog found in Russia. It has thick fur to cope with the cold.

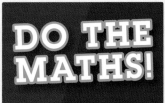

DO THE MATHS!

Use the information in red in the Map-a-stat box to work out the following challenge. How long it would take to ride the entire length of the Trans-Siberian Railway, if you were travelling at a speed of 80 km per hour? Round up your answer. Here is the equation to help you solve the problem.

$$9{,}289 \text{ km} \div 80 \text{ km per hour} = ? \text{ hours}$$

Complete the maths challenge, then turn to pages 28—29 to see if your calculation is correct!

The Middle East

The Middle East is a region in southwest Asia and northern Africa. The Asian countries that tend to be included in this region are Syria, Turkey, Lebanon, Israel, Jordan, Saudi Arabia, Iraq, Iran, Yemen, Oman, United Arab Emirates, Qatar, Bahrain and Kuwait. Sometimes, other countries are included in this region, too, such as Afghanistan and Pakistan.

Human geography

The people who live in the Middle East region have a great deal of cultural and **ethnic diversity**. People's lifestyles are often affected by their surroundings. People living in areas with grazing land tend to raise **livestock**. Those living on the long coasts of the region, or along its rivers, may depend on fishing to make a living. Cities also rise up in areas with more **resources**. The Middle East region is a large producer of oil so many people work in this industry, as well.

Petra, in Jordan, is an ancient city that was partly carved out of rock.

Abu Dhabi is the capital of the United Arab Emirates.

Map-a-stat

Israel has a strip of coastline that is only around 185 km (115 miles) long. Much of the coastline is narrow, but it widens to about 40 km (25 miles) in the south of the country.

The Arabian Peninsula is bordered by the Red Sea on the west and southwest. The Arabian Sea borders it to the south and the southeast. The Persian Gulf and the Gulf of Oman border it to the east. Turkey has a border on the Black Sea, and Iran has a coast on the Caspian Sea.

Engineers maintain water pipes in Ashkelon, Israel.

DO THE MATHS!

Use the information in red in the Map-a-stat box to work out the following challenge. If you were to walk the length of Israel's coastline at a rate of 3.2 km per hour, how long would it take you to complete your journey? Here is the equation to help you solve the problem.

$$185 \text{ km} \div 3.2 \text{ km per hour} = ? \text{ hours}$$

Complete the maths challenge, then turn to pages 28–29 to see if your calculation is correct!

Rivers and lakes

There are many rivers and lakes in Asia. Some of the main rivers are the Ganges, the Lena River, the Indus River, the Mekong River, the Ob River and the Yangtze and Yellow Rivers. The Ganges is sacred to Hindus in India, and also provides food and water for those who live on its banks. It is 2,510 km (1,560 miles) long. The Lena, the Ob and the Yenisei Rivers are in Siberia and flow into the Arctic Ocean. The Yangtze and Yellow Rivers are the longest rivers in China.

Large lakes

Asia is home to two of the world's largest lakes. Lake Baikal, in Siberia, is the oldest freshwater lake on Earth and is also the largest freshwater lake by volume. The Caspian Sea in western Asia is the largest salt lake by area. It has a surface area of 386,400 sq km (149,200 sq miles).

Yenisei River

Lena River

Ob River

Lake Baikal

Yangtze River

Yellow River

Indus River

Mekong River

Ganges River

Lake Baikal is home to more than 1,500 animal species and hundreds of plants.

Map-a-stat

The Yangtze is the longest river in Asia at 6,301 km (3,915 miles) long. It is the third-longest river in the world.

Lake Baikal holds around 20 per cent of the world's freshwater and is 1,620 m (5,315 ft.) deep. More than 330 rivers and streams flow into Lake Baikal.

people washing in the Ganges

The Yellow River is the third-longest river in Asia and the sixth-longest in the world.

the Caspian Sea

DO THE MATHS!

Use the information in red in the Map-a-stat box to work out the following challenge. How long would it take to sail the Yangtze River at a rate of 4.8 km per hour? Round your answer. Here is the equation to help you solve the problem.

$$6,301 \text{ km} \div 4.8 \text{ km per hour} = ? \text{ hours}$$

Complete the maths challenge, then turn to pages 28—29 to see if your calculation is correct!

An amazing continent

Asia is an amazing continent. It has rainforests and deserts, tropical beaches and cold tundra. It also has **modern** cities and small villages. Asia has the tallest mountains, the biggest lakes and the longest coastline of all continents on Earth. It has access to many natural resources and many of its countries have fast-growing economies.

Place of riches

The continent covers a large geographic area and so it has an amazing diversity of habitats and biomes. It also has an amazing range of cultures, religions and political beliefs. In fact, Asia was the birthplace of most of the major world religions. While these differences sometimes lead to conflicts in the area, they also give the continent an incredible richness.

This statue is part of Singapore's oldest Hindu temple, called Sri Mariamman.

Shanghai, China, sits at the mouth of the Yangtze River.

Map-a-stat

Islam is the most commonly practiced religion in Asia. About 25 per cent of the population is Muslim.

Hinduism is the second-most practiced religion in Asia. Buddhism is the third-most practiced religion.

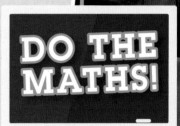

Buddhist monk

Mumbai is on the west coast of India.

DO THE MATHS!

Use the information in red in the Map-a-stat box to work out the following challenge. What percentage of people in Asia are non-Muslim? Here is the equation to help you solve the problem.

$$100 \text{ per cent} - 25 \text{ per cent} = ? \text{ per cent}$$

Complete the maths challenge, then turn to pages 28–29 to see if your calculation is correct!

Maths
challenge
answers

You have made it through the mathalon!
How did your maths skills measure up?
Check your answers below.

DO THE MATHS!

Page 5

100 per cent - 97 per cent
= 3 per cent in Europe

Page 7

4,400,000,000 people –
(1,400,000,000 + 1,200,000,000 people)
= 1,800,000,000 people

Page 9

4,548 m + 2,695 m = 7,243 m
That is shorter than 7,439 m

Page 11

1) 10,200 – 8,850 m = 1,350 m
2) 8,850 m – 4,205 m = 4,645 m

Page 13

45 °C – (-40 °C) = 45 °C + 40 °C
= 85 °C difference in temperature

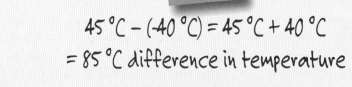

Page 15

8,047 km – 4,828 km
= 3,219 km wider

Page 17

318,000,000 people – 254,000,000 people
= 64,000,000 more people

Page 19

364,485 sq km + 13,430 sq km
= 377,915 sq km

Page 21

9,289 km ÷ 80 km per hour = about 116 hours

Page 23

185 km ÷ 3.2 km per hour = 57.8 hours

Page 25

6,301 km ÷ 4.8 km per hour
= 1,313 hours

Page 27

100 per cent – 25 per cent
= 75 per cent

Glossary

amphibian cold-blooded animal that spends part of its life in water and part on land

archipelago group of island

biodiverse having a large number of different types of living thing in a certain habitat

biome area that has similar plants and animals

climate the kind of weather a certain area has

continent one of Earth's seven large landmasses

culture beliefs, practices and arts of a group of people

cyclone severe storm with a strong wind that blows in a circular pattern

dated eruption report historical report of volcanic eruption

diversity large variety of different types or sorts

economy system of how money is made and used within a particular region or country

ethnic relating to a group of people who have the same race, nationality, beliefs and ways of living

fertile describes ground that is rich and able to produce crops and other plants

geography weather, land, countries, people and businesses in a particular area or region

geological relating to Earth's rocks and minerals

grassland large area of land covered by grass

habitat surrounding area where animals or plants naturally live

isthmus narrow strip of land that connects two larger bodies of land

landmass huge area of land

livestock farm animal, such as cattle and sheep, kept for its meat, wool or skin

metropolitan area very large, heavily populated urban area, including all of its suburbs

modern using the most up-to-date ideas or ways of doing things

monsoon season season in some areas that has heavy rains called monsoon rains

permafrost soil or earth that stays frozen all year round

reptile animal that has scales covering its body and that uses the sun to control its body temperature

resource something that people need to live, such as fuel or food

species single kind of living thing. All people are one species.

steppe grassland with few trees or bushes

subtropical desert type of desert that is hot and dry all year round

summit highest point of a mountain

tectonic plate moving piece of Earth's crust, the top layer of Earth

tropical rainforest rainforest that is found near the equator

tsunami very large, destructive wave, an usually caused by undersea earthquake or eruption

tundra cold, treeless plain that often has permanently frozen soil

Find out more

Books

Adventures Around the Globe, Lonely Planet Kids
(Lonely Planet, 2015)

Asia: Everything You Ever Wanted to Know (Not for Parents)
(Lonely Planet, 2014)

China (Countries in Our World), Oliver James
(Franklin Watts, 2013)

Introducing Asia (Introducing Continents), Anita Ganeri
(Raintree, 2014)

Russia (Countries in Our World), Galya Ransome
(Franklin Watts, 2012)

Websites

Learn fun facts about Asia at:
www.activityvillage.co.uk/asia

Find out more about Asia at:
www.timeforkids.com/around-the-world

Find a lot of great websites about Asia at:
**uk.wow.com/search?s_pt=aolsem&s_it=aolsem&s_
    chn=61&q=asia%20fact%20for%20kids**

Index